I0201412

HOW TO TRANSITION

A Single Mother's Guide to Coping With Change

by
Rebecca Travis

No parts of this book may be used or reproduced by any means, graphic, electronic, or mechanical, including photocopying, recording, taping or by any information storage retrieval system without the written permission of the author except in the case of brief quotations embodied in critical articles and reviews.

This book may be ordered through booksellers or by contacting:

iGlobal Educational Services, LLC
PO Box 94224
Phoenix, Arizona 85070
www.iglobaleducation.com
512-761-5898

Because of the dynamic nature of the Internet, any web addresses or links contained in this book may have changed since publication and may no longer be valid. The views expressed in this work are solely those of the author and do not necessarily reflect the views of the publisher, and the publisher hereby disclaims any responsibility for them.

This is a work of fiction. Names, characters, businesses, places, events, and incidents are either the products of the author's imagination or used in a fictitious manner. Any resemblance to actual persons, living or dead, or actual events is purely coincidental.

HOW TO TRANSITION:
A Single Mother's Guide to Coping with Change

Copyright © 2017 iGlobal Educational Services.
All Rights Reserved.

ISBN-13: 978-1-944346-79-9

Dedication

I would like to dedicate this book to my son, whose smile that wakes me every morning reminds me of how much good this journey has provided for me despite its saddening circumstances. May the smiles of your children remind you of your strength.

Table of Contents

Chapter One:
COPING

It's happened.

That dreaded "D" word has finally come to fruition.

Whether you title it a "discharge," "dissolution," or "divorce," it is a catastrophic event that demolishes a foundation someone assumed was permanent. The event brings anger, tears, depression, and even hatred into a relationship that once blossomed with love, flourished with memories, and outlined itself in late-night conversations as the two parties involved postulated about the future and eventual steps towards their dream career.

Somewhere along the way, however, something changed.

Now, the couch has a permanent indent from where you have been sitting up late at night, wondering how in the world you are going to get through this. You think about your children, sound asleep in their rooms as they dream their worlds away, and you wonder how you are going to feed them.

Clothe them.

Insure them.

Reassure them.

Split their precious time with your soon-to-be ex-spouse.

Some of these scenarios do not apply to every situation. In some cases, someone is fleeing abuse, in which case you hope you will *never* have to split the children's time with the other party. Some soon-to-be single mothers already have jobs, and now it is an issue of finding the right day care on such short notice. Maybe you are a mother sitting on the couch with your spouse's threats running through your mind. Maybe you are a mom that has experienced threats from your spouse of taking your children away, for whatever reason they can orchestrate.

If you are reading this book, and any one of these scenarios fits you, then it's time to start the very first step in a long line of successive moments that will define who you will become in the eyes of your children, and in the eyes of the world.

It is time to cope.

The first step in coping is identifying your emotions. It is all right to feel anything you are currently feeling. Women who have been cheated on feel anger, resentment, and lower self-esteem as they try to figure out what she wasn't doing to make her spouse happy. Women who have been left simply because the spouse was tired feel sadness, depression, anger, and a host of other emotions that come with dealing with the absence of a loved one.

The truth of the matter is that you are grieving a death: the death of a relationship that has been there for years. The death of a relationship that defined who you were. Stepping into crowds, you would introduce yourself as so-and-so's spouse before giving your name, like a royal title of "Duchess" or "Queen." Or, maybe you gave your name first before stating who your spouse was, like the abbreviated acronyms for degrees achieved after years of work invested into a particular subject.

The subject of your spouse.

Coping is more than just the eventual "getting over" of emotions. It is also the identification of those emotions as well as their root causes. Anger, yes, but anger over what? Sadness, yes, but grieving over what? Hatred, possibly, but what do you hate? Yes, sometimes the clear-and-true answer is "your spouse," but often the issue runs much deeper than that. Women who have been cheated on are not just angry at their spouse for stepping out of the marriage, they are angry at the lie. They are angry at their inability to catch it. Or, maybe they knew something was going on, but they are angry at not calling their spouse on it sooner.

Women who are fleeing abusive relationships are depressed, yes. But, their depression and anger can be over many things: anger at not uprooting and leaving sooner, depression at the idea of subjecting their children to that kind of lifestyle. Even sadness at the stigma that still comes with people fleeing abusive relationships and what that 'must say about their personality.'

Emotions are not triggered, they are rooted. It is only when that root is exposed, like a nerve, that the emotion begins to bubble into existence. Providing a metaphorical manifestation to a stark chemical reaction taking place in the brain enables our conscious mind to process the events currently unfolding. It is hard to shake an emotion, but it is easier to do when there is a root cause that has to be resolved.

Then, and only then, can you begin to move forward. It is not enough to allow yourself to experience the emotion. Its root cause also must be identified, confronted, and processed.

For some, the marriage has been struggling for a while. For those mothers under a constant daily struggle for survival, divorce can seem like a way to finally breathe. For others, it is a shock to the system as your mind scrambles to figure out what you did wrong. You begin telling yourself that had you done something else different, or better-- or more—then this would not have happened. But, here is the truth: it takes two to make a marriage, and it takes two to break a marriage. If one spouse is finished and no longer willing to make it work, then there is nothing the other party can do.

And that is usually the hardest pill of all to swallow.

So, you cope. You identify your emotions, you filter through to their root cause, and you confront them head-on so that you can be mentally, emotionally, and spiritually prepared for supporting your children through this tumultuous time.

And then? You plan.

Planning is essential to the coping process because it enables you to take this entire transition and break it down into bite-sized chunks that are easier to swallow. Your mind begins whirling with financial questions, homeowner questions, schooling questions, career questions, and even paperwork questions. You begin to wonder where you will live and whether your children will be properly educated in the surrounding school system. You remember that little Johnny is going through a growth spurt and your mind begins to run furious calculations and suddenly, you remember you haven't been in the workforce for a certain number of years, and pretty soon you're slumped over a pint of ice cream or a bottle of wine at midnight as your heart beats heavily against your chest.

Do not worry.

This book will take you through how to break up those chunks and formulate a plan. It might not be a perfect plan, but it is a plan that will get you from your immediate Point A to your immediate Point B.

Because sailing through a separation and divorce is the same as motherhood: you take it one day at a time.

Reflection Questions:

1. What can you do to stay strong for your children?
2. How can you work in giving yourself moments during the day to sit and think?

Chapter Two:
SEPARATION

When the initial separation occurs, a new phase needs to be addressed. Whether the two of you still slept in the same bed or in different beds in the house, getting used to the dynamic of not having them around can be rough. No matter the situation, there is always the stark feeling of change, and that can bring about swirling thoughts and fears regarding a future that is no longer defined.

When you have something to occupy your time, such as a spouse, a job, children, or a dirty home, it's easy to push your own thoughts to the side. It's easy to think you are coping well because of the unacknowledged emotions that are swimming around in your head. But, when that first round of true silence happens, the party in question is always proven wrong. Soon, those nap times become moments for emotional upheaval, and those nights where you lay in an empty bed and stare at the ceiling go from mumbling lowly about your spouse in the basement to wondering how you might defend yourself if someone decides to force themselves into your home.

This transition is fear-inducing, and it isn't to be taken lightly.

What you are feeling is normal. Even if you are someone who has felt the gap in your marriage for quite some time, and even if you are someone who has long since felt love for your soon-to-be ex-spouse, it doesn't make this transition any harder. Watching them come and go from the house while they gather their things doesn't get any easier.

And if it isn't easy for you, think about what it is doing to your children.

Here is the truth: you must find a way to stay civil with your spouse during this transition. It will be easier to stay civil when the two of you are having one phone call a week with regard to the children, but it is much harder to stay civil face-to-face during this time of pulling apart finances, filling out paperwork, and personally divvying up time with the children.

But, it is no longer about you and what you want.

Whether you are the one moving from the home and into another place of residence or the one still in the original home, understand that the trauma of watching a parent permanently leave the house is one that will not easily erase from a child's mind. This means the two of you have to coordinate when the spouse leaving is going to come by for their things. They cannot just "drop by," and it isn't good for the children to be there when it is happening.

The best times are while the children are in school. If the transitioning is happening on a weekend, call up a mother-friend and see if she can babysit your children at her place for a couple of hours. There are ways to work with your spouse so they can get their things without the children having to see the hustling and bustling.

And, let's face it, it's going to take a while to learn how to be civil. No matter the cause of the separation or whose "fault" it is, being civil with one another takes as much practice as living together was when you were first married.

If you and your spouse are level-headed enough to agree on a dissolution, then I applaud you. Many couples that decide to call off their marriage cannot agree on anything, and it makes it that much harder on children in the long run, especially when the custody battle arises. While a dissolution takes much less time and doesn't require a period of separation, that does not mean that separation does not happen. Whether someone moves out or the two parties simply stop depending on the other, it will never be the same. Your thoughts will still rear their heads late at night or during periods of silence, and you will find yourself easily overwhelmed.

Do not fight these times, because these times will be necessary for you. It is imperative that you keep a level-head in front of your children, because they will be looking to you for answers, guidance, and strength. It is in these silent times, when no one is around, that you will be able to filter through emotions, contemplate toward self-actualization, and begin to cope with the things happening in your life.

Do not let your children see you spin out of control. Why? Because this time of drastic change requires as much routine as possible. Keeping their lives as normal as possible is going to help them cope independently. You cannot allow your emotions to swallow you when your children are looking to you for stability, comfort, and answers.

Through all of this, keep the well-being of your children at the forefront of your priorities.

Another thing to keep in mind during this entire process is making sure not to degrade their other parent in front of them. You might no longer love your spouse, but they still love their other parent. It is emotionally detrimental to a child to speak poorly of their other parent while they are around in any capacity. On another note, just because your spouse no longer wants to be married does not mean they want to abandon their children. It is your job as the co-parent to not only hold your tongue, but to actively encourage them to maintain a kosher relationship with the other parent.

Because this isn't just about you.

If they ask you questions, note that it is in their best interest to know the truth, so be honest and gentle. Sometimes a situation is too difficult to understand, or too painful to recount, or maybe you fear it might damage your ex-spouse's relationship with their children. Maybe you feel their questions are better answered by the other party, so a subtler answer is required.

The perfect answer in these scenarios is: "Love does not equal compatibility."

Outside of extreme circumstances, that is essentially what happened. You loved one another, married, dreamed of a life together, and then over time the two parties involved grew incompatible. For older children who understand the world around them better, you can be the judge as to whether or not they can handle the truth. But, for children who are younger and confused and looking to you for guidance, that answer is both succinct, easy to explain, and leaves out the murky details.

Above all, do not lie to your children. No matter what age, and no matter what mental faculties they may or may not possess, never convince yourself it is alright to lie. They are going through enough right now. They don't need to try and cope with the fact that they are now being lied to about one of the most influential experiences of their life.

This is going to be a hard process. Staying civil with your spouse, separating personal possessions into two separate homes, and coming up with a cohesive schedule for the children's time until the court date is going to be hard. But, throughout all of it, it is imperative to keep these three things in mind: never demean your spouse in front of your children, never lie to them, and keep their well-being at the forefront of your mind. These three ideas will enable you to make the best decisions available to you no matter the emotional state-of-mind you find yourself in.

Because this isn't about you. Not anymore.

Reflection Questions:

1. What answers will you give your children as they begin asking questions? How will you stay honest with them?
2. How can you stay headstrong with your spouse so you are not manipulated?

Chapter Three:
A NEW HOME

Leaving a home you've known for so long can induce all sorts of typical emotions: fear, loss, sadness, anguish. It can become a stressful time in someone's life when they begin to branch out and leave what they know for something they are not familiar with. Maybe your situation is not requiring you to move out of the state, or even out of the city, in which you reside. Maybe you are able to keep the home you are currently in while your ex-spouse is responsible for finding another home. But, there is still a massive dynamic within the home that changes its definition, and that is the absence of a parent. A life-long partner. A lover.

And sometimes, that absence can trigger unresolved emotions.

For some, there is a complete split on both ends. Sometimes, one spouse finds another place in the same area and the mother takes the children back to her home state to be surrounded by family. For others, the ex-spouse is staying in the original home while you take them elsewhere. Maybe you are fleeing to a domestic shelter for those fleeing an abusive relationship, or maybe you are going and staying with a friend temporarily until you can figure out your next move.

No matter the scenario, the definition of "home" has changed, and with that comes new and unresolved emotions that can cause turmoil for both you and your children.

The first emotion that will arise is fear. There is a great deal of uncertainty before finding your next move with your children, and it can induce a state of panic. In this stage, communication with your children is not as imperative as most make it seem. In this stage, where there are no answers to questions until you can research and make some calls, what you must be able to do is find a way to cope with your panic in a way that your children do not bear witness.

What I mean is this: if the children ask what is going on, tell them that mom and dad are just trying to work on some things. Because, that is what is happening, right? Remember, lying to your children is not a smart thing to do, but when you do not have any answers for them, even vague is better than a lie. They will know something is happening, and it is up to you to not only reassure them everything will be alright, but that you have everything under control.

Some ways to cope with panic are certain breathing techniques. When you find yourself becoming overwhelmed with a task at hand, the first step is to back away from what is happening. Then, close your eyes, and slowly begin breathing through your nose. Focus on your thoughts and what is swirling around in your head. What made you panic? Was it a thought? A realization? An emotion? Pinpointing the point of panic will enable you to resolve it rather than pushing it off to the side. Through all of this, keeping a strong stance with your children does not mean neglecting yourself. It means strategically aiding yourself in any way possible when the main focus is not your children.

This could mean everything from when they are at school to when they are sleeping. Your time for you is when they are not a priority in your immediate view. That is when you will be able to cope.

And you need to.

After the initial panic of uncertainty, plans will slowly begin to fall into place, and for many this is where emotions begin to divert. If you are a mother with a job, obtaining a new home might not be that big of a challenge. If you are a mother with no income and no job experience, finding a new home is much more difficult. And, with this difficulty can come the want to ask for advice. But, that advice usually comes with phone calls that should be made, and with these phone calls come conversations and questions from the other party. It can drudge up buried and deep-seated emotions just simply attempting to answer their questions, and this is where you have a choice to make: you can confide in someone, or you can close yourself off.

Either decision is fine, and here is why: coping with this transition is less about leaning on someone and more about finding a place to stay. The urgency of needing a place to take your children trumps the idea of emotionally leaning on someone. With that said, this does not mean you cannot lean on someone. It simply means that if you choose not to, this does not make you a bad person. It simply means you are compartmentalizing one task at a time.

That is how some people cope and deal with impending situations with multiple steps like this one, and that is fine.

But, once you have arrangements made, this brings on another plate of emotions. Now, you have a place where you are going. Whether that place is permanent or temporary, it brings about an imperative goal: communicating this move with your children.

If your children are younger, this part is less about verbal communication and more about physical communication. For any child of any age, once they have become rooted in familiar scenarios, moving can be a big emotional disruption for them. It is why a multitude of books have been written on the importance of routine within a young child's life. In order to combat this upheaval of emotions, the best thing you could do is pack while they are asleep. Keep the bags within your room, and shut the door so they cannot get in. Keep their outer surroundings within their current home as stable as possible.

If bigger things, such as furniture and televisions, will be moved before you can leave with your children, then find a way to make it fun for them. For example, if your ex-spouse is taking the couches and leaving you the beds, then bring the beds into the main room. It will be odd to your child at first, but when they realize you can have movie marathons on the television with popcorn while laying right in bed, the change will no longer matter to them.

For older children, it becomes a trickier situation to navigate. If your children are older and understand the idea of broader concepts, then it becomes less about distracting them from the situation and more about communicating it. During this transition, your child will have many questions, and I advise you to answer them as honestly as you can. Despite your raging emotions, a young child's way of coping with new circumstances is to learn all they can about it. Do not get frustrated, and stay patient. In any scenario, it is possible to make the transition fun. If you are traveling states away to find a new home, book a hotel along the way for an evening and let your children swim. If you are moving only a few hours away, but back in with your parents, tell them you are going to spend some time with grandma and grandpa. Get them in on the action and see if grandma will cook an awesome meal the first night in. Maybe grandpa wouldn't mind taking the kids to a movie that night.

If your transition consists of moving from an abusive home and into a transition home, whether that home is with a friend, family member, or a shelter, the first thing you need to do is applaud yourself. Look yourself in the mirror, take a deep breath, and tell yourself how incredible and strong you are.

Then, find ways to make this transition fun for your children.

If you are staying with a friend, celebrate that fact. Ask if your friend buy a cake for the kids to snack on when you get there. Give them something to look forward to. If you are heading to a shelter, whether you had some time to pack or not, there are still ways to make the transition fun and entertaining for your children. Have a pajama party and pile into bed and sleep together while you hold them close. This action will not only help you cope with the present situation, it will make your children feel safe as well as give them the sense that they are at a party. If you were able to grab a few of their toys, play an imaginary game with them. Some shelters organize events for children within the building, so take advantage of that and take them to participate in some of them. These activities are built to do one thing: distract and enable fun during a difficult scenario and transition.

And that is exactly what has to happen during this separative transition.

Reflection Questions:

1. How can you celebrate the little milestones in this process?
2. Have you found someone you can vent to emotionally?

Chapter Four:
ALL ABOUT YOUR CHILDREN

A s an adult, you will have more coping processes than children. Because you have lived a longer life, you have developed more precise ways of coping with circumstances that are sometimes beyond your control. However, your children have not. This is why it is imperative to understand that this process is no longer about you. You have developed. You are done growing. You have experienced things in life that have led you to find ways to process, sift through, and cope with scenarios.

Your children, however, have not.

It is not because you are not important, and it is not because you are not being affected. It is because your children are not as developed as you, and this event can impact them in ways that will change the course of their development forever.

This is not being said to make you back out of your decision. This is simply being said to make sure you understand that you *are* important, there are just other variables in play that have to be sorted out first.

Children at different ages react in different ways. If your children are younger than four, then the process is less about explanation and more about distraction. The average human mind does not begin recalling specific events and memories until the age of 5, so it is very possible that your child will not remember the actual divorce. This can be both a blessing and a curse, because it does lead to questions down the road as they grow older that might be painful to answer. Remember, never lie to your children, but understand that their minds can only process so much. There is always a way to frame the truth so they can understand it.

And, if you are caught off-guard with these questions, the phrase "love does not equal compatibility" is always a great one to begin with.

With older children who might be able to recall this scenario, somewhere between the ages of 5 and 7, the distraction is not as important. What is important here is making sure the transition is kept as much out of their eyes as possible. If things have to be shuffled and a spouse comes to pick up their things, arrange it during their school time or while they are at a friend's on the weekend. There is no greater impact on a child than watching one of their parents leave. Remember when you would try to walk out of the house and the child would scream for you to come back? That instinct does not go away just because they grow older.

That instinct merely becomes internalized.

With teenagers, the most important part of this process is making sure questions they have are answered. Be honest about the transition happening, and include them in the process. This does not mean asking them what parent they want to live with, but it means asking them how they feel, talking about how they might want to arrange their room in a new place, or simply asking them if there is anything they want to say about it. Just like you have emotions you wish to air out somehow, older children will have the same thing. And sometimes, they will feel more compelled to go to their friends and talk than to come to you. That is fine. What is important for them is that they have the ability to talk through this and cope with this in their own ways.

But, there is something you have to do with older children that is not always required with younger children, and that is reminding them that this is not their fault.

Children have ways of blaming themselves for things that stems from what we ingrain in them as babies. We try to teach our children to take responsibility for their actions and their consequences by instilling punishments, such as timeouts and the taking away of toys. But, as they grow older, that instillation of responsibility begins branching out. As they begin to take responsibility for their actions, they also start to interpret the world around them. As their brains begin to grow and things such as linear thinking begin to evolve, their perception of the world changes.

This means that the way they perceive the consequences of their actions changes.

As a baby, their idea of action and consequence stems from something they actually do: throw a cheerio off the side of the high chair and watch what it does. Throwing the cheerio is the action and it falling is the consequence. However, once they get older, their literal interpretation of the world begins to expand, and their idea of action and consequence goes from "action and reaction" to "attitude and consequence."

Why? Because teenagers have attitudes fueled by hormones, and those attitudes are the next "stage" to tackle.

So, when a teenager knows they are being punished for their attitudes at times, they interpret the leaving of a parent with their mood swings because the "action" is their attitude and the "consequence" they see happening is the parent leaving.

This is why reassuring them that this is not their fault is imperative, because teenagers see the world differently than they did when they were merely a toddler.

There are always ways to reassure children of all ages that things will be alright, and one of them stems around equal time with the parents. Now, if you are a mother pulling yourself and your children out of an abusive situation, then do not fret this part. But, if you are a mother pulling away from a marriage with a spouse who is not abusive, then this part is crucial, no matter your personal feelings towards them: each parent is important to a child's development in some way. Now, maybe you are a mother who has lost a spouse, and this is not something that is reasonable. First of all, I am so very sorry for your loss.

But, if you are a mother who is going through a separation and divorce with a spouse who is not abusive, then understand that your personal feelings do not dictate whether or not the other spouse will have access to their children. Your children are not pawns in your emotional game, and making them pawns will only jeopardize your own children's health and well-being. Finding a way to establish equal time between both parents until a custody agreement can be arranged is imperative, and it takes a great deal of maturity in order to be able to organize it.

But it is for the benefit of your children, and that is more important than your personal outlook on your spouse.

Other ways to reassure your children that everything will be alright is keeping them on as much of a routine as possible. The less deviation they have from their days, the better off they will be. Routines ground us, and sometimes a simple missed cup of coffee can throw off our entire day for hours. Children work the same way.

However, a little indulgence on their part is not completely out of the picture. Find a random weekend to take the kids out on a day-trip. It will help get your mind off of things and get them out of the house to explore. Sometimes distraction is good for everyone.

Even though it does not feel like it right now, you will make it out of this scenario just fine. You will find your footing and your new way of life, and you will settle into a new routine with a new "normal." However, your children do not have those coping skills yet, and it will be imperative for your to help them find theirs. Make sure you do not sink so far into your own mind that you neglect the fact that your children need you now more than ever.

How To Transition

Reflection Questions:

1. What type of steady routine are your children on right now? Is it a routine they are familiar with?
2. How are you answering your children when they have questions?
3. Are you still remembering to breathe?

Chapter Five:
FINDING A NEW CAREER

For many single mothers, finding a job is the hardest task to tackle. Some have not been in the workforce for as long as a decade, and some even more. It can be hard to look through job description after job description and pass them all by when you begin to realize that you do not fit all of the requirements necessary for that basic secretarial job.

It can be debilitating, and it can make you question whether or not you are making the right decision for your life.

The truth of the matter is that 72% of women who advocate for divorce end up staying because of financial reasons. Women still earn $0.70 to every $1.00 earned by a man, and women are more likely to be passed over for promotions if a man is vying for the same position, despite qualifications. The United States has not seen progression of minimum wage in decades despite the fact that costs of living in every state skyrocket as much as 5% every single year, and this is what leads to many single mothers working bottom-of-the-barrel jobs and living in government-subsidized housing simply to put a roof over her children's heads.

And that prospect is terrifying to a woman.

But, you might have more job experience than you realize. That volunteer work? It counts as experience. Just because you did not get paid for it does not mean it can't go down on a resume. Add the work you did for the homeless shelter! Count the work you did at your church! Did you lead a bible study? Did you volunteer at your child's school? Did you help pick up trash alongside a road? Did you volunteer to be the neighborhood dog walker? Did you babysit for someone? All of these types of credentials can be written down onto a resume not only as work experience, but as references for your work ethic.

If you are a mother who did not have the time for volunteer work, do not fret. The work you have done as a mother does count. Things such as time management, patience, cooperation, multi-tasking, and other skills that come with being a mother are pertinent in the workplace. Simply list the last job you did have, and then begin listing various skill sets. Talk about your education, if you have any. Talk about those skills that make you unique. Talk about those multi-tasking and organizational skills. A resume is not the end-all-be-all of job hunting. It is supposed to be a physical manifestation of you as a person. A resume is not supposed to sell you for the job, it is supposed to get you in the door for an interview so that *you* can sell you for the job.

For mothers that have limited experience in both volunteer work and other areas, there will be a point where you will have to work any job that comes along. However, federal programs are in place for a reason. No, it is not a way of life, but it is a means to an end to help in tough situations like this one. Food assistance can mean the difference between paying rent or not, and help with paying a gas bill during the winter months can mean the difference between paying the water bill or not.

Understand that the first job you take does not have to be the last. Any job experience is going to look wonderful on a resume, even if that job experience is only six months. If all you can find is a night-shift position, then the first move you could make is vying for one of their daytime positions. From there, you build skills that will transfer well into other jobs, and after a year at a job you can potentially be in a good position to interview for other jobs that might suit you a bit better.

Just because you might have to scrape the bottom of the barrel does not mean you have to settle. Your children will be watching your every move, and they will see how hard you are working. But, they will also see your unhappiness. Do not stay in a position you are unhappy with simply because you do not feel you have chances elsewhere. This is where proactivity is going to become the new normal. Staying proactive in your place of work, no matter where it is, will always look good on someone. With the proactivity comes acknowledgement from a boss, which turns into a glowing reference, and can sometimes even lead to a promotion where you might be better suited and happier overall.

Whether you believe it or not, your happiness is paramount in this situation. Yes, it is not just about you, but that does not mean that this isn't about you at all. Your happiness, your health, and your self-worth are even more important now, especially when your children are watching you are much as they are. This is why taking care of yourself in every aspect, including a job-related aspect, is tantamount to taking care of your children and making sure they are alright.

Because you are the glue holding everything together during this process.

Reflection Questions:

1. What about your role in your children's lives has shifted?
2. How can you utilize all your resources to find a job?
3. Have you created a clear path for your goals for the future?

Chapter Six:
KEEPING YOURSELF HEALTHY

Just like any stressor in life, divorce is an event that brings about many different issues. For some, it is an emotional rollercoaster. For others, it is a constant mental battle to figure out what happened. For some, it devolves into a fight between keeping on a forward trajectory and succumbing to the turmoil an event like that brings. Children rely on their parents for everything well into their later years of development, and more so in moments like these. Just as this point in your life is confusing, angering, and saddening for you, so it is for your children as well. This is why keeping yourself healthy is of the utmost importance.

Throughout this entire book, we have been talking about the idea of your children coming first, and yes, that idea is imperative to understand. But, studies have shown us time after time that children are more receptive as visual learners than they are oral learners. This is why parents are always stressed to lead a life they are proud of, because their children learn from what they see their parents do. In this regard, simply telling your children it will be alright and that they will be fine is not enough. They have to see it from you. They need to see that you are fine and that you are alright.

This is why taking care of your health is imperative. As a mother, whether single or married, there is a false expectation to sacrifice your entire self for your children. This creates mental and emotional dichotomies that lead many mothers to anxiety and mood disorders, and can even spawn serious mental illnesses such as severe depression. Just as your children need to be taken care of, so do you. The difference, however, is that it is your job to take care of yourself as well, not just your children's.

Mental, physical, and emotional health are the three main categories of health are measured by doctors. All three harbor incredible successes when taken care of, and massive downfalls when not. When mental health suffers, the chemical imbalances in the brain wreak havoc on emotional states, which can lead to things such as the musculature breakdown of tissues and early deterioration of bones. When emotional health suffers, it can prompt unhealthy mental thoughts that lead to outward physical issues, such as weight loss, weight gain, and even self-harm. And, if physical health is neglected, both mental and emotional health take a turn for the worst because the body no longer feels capable of efficient production, and it can lead to unhealthy chemical imbalances that trigger things such as separation anxiety and bipolar disorders. Keeping yourself healthy in these three areas will keep your children healthy because not only will you be setting an example, you will also have the energy to keep up with them when they are not taking care of themselves.

And, trust me, a time will come when they are not taking care of themselves.

Taking care of your mental state means allowing time to relax. Breathing exercises, meditation, and even the occasional nap will go a long way in preserving your mental state. If long, hot showers are something that settle you down, work one into your routine. If a hot cup of coffee helps calm you nerves, find some time to settle down and have one. You are about to embark on a lifestyle that, while rewarding, comes with a great deal of stress. Find ways to alleviate it now and make them a habit so you do not struggle with stress-induced health issues in the future.

Preserving your emotional health is paramount. Being able to handle your own children's emotional upheavals means having patience and understanding, and it is hard to be patient when you are worn down emotionally as well. If you are someone who enjoys those hot baths and showers, take the time to cry. If your children are at school or having fun at a sleepover, take the time to scream. Hunker down with a cup of coffee or a glass of wine, call a friend, and rant. Take some time to spew whatever emotional baggage is necessary in any way you see fit. For some people, this means exercising. For other people, this means talking. For others, it means watching emotional movies in order to promote the crying process. Emotional health for you, as a budding single mother, is imperative because of the patience it affords you to help your children with their own emotional states.

Your physical health, however, is arguably the most important aspect of health. If taken advantage of or somehow abused, it can spawn other physical illnesses that will drain you of your emotional and mental well-being. Keeping as close to a nutritious diet as possible will help with those moments of fatigue that will happen because of the coping and expelling of swells of emotion. Getting out and taking a long walk will help you get out from underneath the weight of the world crushing down on you, and it will help realign your negative trains of thought. But, that movement will also ward off musculature disintegration and stiff joints. Keeping your body filled with the nutrients it needs will enable your body to produce the energy stores you will need in order to be a single parent. It takes a substantial amount of energy to embark on this new path, and your body needs to be ready.

Other ways to stay on top of these three aspects of health are listening to music, getting a bit more sleep, removing your partner's stuff from your eyesight, meditation, and finding a group of mothers who are in the same boat as you. There is a lot to be said for like-minded individuals coming together and the comfort and wisdom they bring to the table.

Your health is paramount to the health of your children. Setting an example for them will do more than any command you could give them to follow. Take care of yourself during this time, because it is no one's job to do it for you. Take the time to shave your legs. Take the time to enjoy a second cup of coffee. Go to bed an hour earlier. Set your alarm for an hour later. Find ways to help rid your body, mind, and soul of the stresses bombarding your system because of this moment in your life.

It will serve both you and your children well in the long run.

Reflection Questions:

1. What is your ultimate form of relaxation, and how can you employ that in your everyday life?
2. What aspect of your health are you currently neglecting, and what can you do to make sure you treat that area of your life with care?

Chapter Seven:
STRESS MANAGEMENT

Stress wreaks havoc on our bodies in ways we do not even realize. The chemical that can induce stress (cortisol) is also vital to many functions in our bodies. Everything from prompt immune responses all the way to fluctuating metabolic function all rely on this chemical to help bolster their necessary functions. The adrenal gland is responsible for the production of this chemical, but when its secretions become constant, the adrenal gland has no downtime to rest and repair itself. This results in unwanted side effects due to a fatigued gland and too much cortisol flooding the body, such as chronic migraines, sleep deprivation, and the breakdown of necessary muscular tissues.

Aside from the physical, raging cortisol levels also have a great impact on the brain. Excess cortisol can overstimulate other chemical reactions within the brain, creating imbalances that can trigger everything from depression to lesions on the brain. Then, those lesions disable many neurotransmitters from receiving many of the chemicals necessary for basic emotional functions, which result in unstable and unhealthy emotional responses.

Stress is the single greatest downfall of many individuals, from weight to psychological stability. When doctors ask their patients to promote ways to destress their lives, it is not simply because they feel someone is "wound too tight." It is because they understand the havoc that prolonged stress can wreak on the body if not kept in check. For single mothers, this breakdown of the body is the last thing any wants to deal with. This chemical that can cause so much trouble inwardly will begin to manifest outwardly, from physical signs of neglect to yourself to short fuses with your children. When overly-stressed, more people suffer than simply yourself, your children not only see it but experience and feel your stress and frustration, and it makes a confusing situation that much worse on them.

This is why stress management should be one of the top priorities for single mothers, because if not properly dealt with, stress can cause untimely emotional backlash onto your children and can result in permanently damaging relationships with the people in your life that do care about the situation you are in. Even just taking five minutes out of your day to breathe deeply or enjoy your favorite drink can go a long way in abating the symptoms that arise when too much cortisol floods the body.

For some, having alone time is imperative to relieving stress and tension throughout the body and mind. In this regard, make sure you work in some alone time. Some suggestions are taking a hot shower after all of the children are in bed, getting up 20 minutes earlier to enjoy that first cup of coffee in silence, and working into your budget $20 for a neighborhood babysitter. You do not need a reason to hire someone in the neighborhood to watch your children. Many people will watch children for an hour or two for $20.00, and you can use that time however you wish. It does not mean you are a bad mother and it does not mean you do not love your children. It means that you understand the value of taking care of yourself just as you would take care of your children.

For some, relaxing is being around other individuals. For these moments, finding a babysitter for the evening so you can go have dinner with a fellow friend or even congregating at a house with other mothers and their children have a drastic effect on overall stress levels. Other options are inviting a friend to come over after the children are in bed, having regular evening conversations with someone you trust and respect, and even planning weekend vacations to get you and your children out and about and around other people.

Relieving your stress does not mean you have to have your children around, but what it requires is self-awareness. If a situation that you thought would bring you relaxation is actually causing more stress, remove yourself from it and try again. Sometimes a relaxing situation that we once found therapeutic simply becomes a stark reminder of what we once had, and your emotional coping of the present situation plays into this quite a bit. Find what truly relaxes you and partake it in. It is not an indulgence nor is it something you have to earn. It is a basic foundation for the idea of self-care and it is necessary if you want your lifestyle to have a positive impact on your children instead of a negative one.

Reflection Questions:

1. What helps you to destress on a regular basis? Are there any scenarios, actions, drinks, or breathing techniques that make you smile?
2. How will you implement these techniques into your weekly routine?
3. What are ways you can take these actions or relaxing scenarios and turn them into 5-minute bursts to work into your busy schedule?

Chapter Eight:
YOU ARE MORE IMPORTANT THAN EVER

In a marriage, many people have someone to depend on. Whether they depend on that person to watch the children while they shower or simply depend on that person to pick something up from the store on the way home, there is a dependency level that is no longer there. This adds more things to the schedule of a single mother than any care to admit, and it causes many mothers to allow other things to fall to the wayside, including their grooming habits.

It never starts off as an intentional thing. Maybe a schedule has run late or one of the kids got off early from soccer practice, and it some somehow skewed the schedule you were running on. So, in order to utilize that extra time in a conservative way, other things get shoved into that extra 15 or 20 minutes. Maybe your child getting off early allowed you to run and pick up that gallon of milk you needed, or maybe leaving work late prohibited you from picking up something to cook for dinner before you had to beat the bus home to greet your children. Either way, time either gets filled with other necessities, such as grocery runs and trips to the bank, and lost time falls to the wayside along with other responsibilities we had to ourselves.

Then, it progresses. In order to make up for that lost time the day before, an earlier day has to happen. So, you figure you can forgo a shower just this once in favor of an extra swipe of deodorant and some stronger perfume. You throw your hair up into a proper bun or pin it back with sparkling bobby pins to detract from the two-day old grease in your hair, and away you go.

But, you are doing something you do not realize, and that is setting a habit. This starting habit then morphs into something greater, which is the idea that things you hold near and dear to you can be compromised for "more important" endeavors, and pretty soon you are only showering twice a week and you are lucky if you wash your hair that often. Things like that glass of wine at the end of the day or that bi-monthly manicure appointment are soon things of the past in favor of issues that are "more pertinent," and in the process you are compromising things that make you feel human.

This is not simply about carving time out for yourself, this is also about basic care. Many mothers who go through this transition busy their time and call it "coping" when really all they are doing is running away from something that has happened to them. What they do not want to do is take the time to sit down and process because they are scared of the flood of emotions that will happen, and they are concerned that it will consume them whole.

I am here to tell you that it won't.

I am also hear to tell you that if you are not coping, self-care is going to be close to impossible.

Self-care and basic grooming tactics are all things any person needs. Single, married, children, no children... all humans have the right to basic elements that help them feel good. But, they also have an obligation to take care of the body they are in. Physical, mental, and emotional health is not merely what you do with your spare time, it is also how you treat your body. Brushing your teeth, taking regular showers, and washing your hair are just a few of the grooming techniques employed to not only make someone feel good, but to look professional in the workplace. If you sacrifice those for things that are "more important," than you risk the professional environment you are using to keep your children clothed, fed, and safe.

You are important now more than ever. When your children are with you, they depend solely on you. This means that time management is pertinent. Find ways to utilize your time so that those errands that have to be run do not impede on things that help you feel womanly and human. It is not a crime to enjoy a quiet cup of coffee nor is it a crime to enjoy a movie after hours. What is a crime, and what will brew the frustrations ultimately taken out on your children, is neglecting basic things because you feel it is your job as a mother.

Your children will learn from you visually before they will ever listen to you. If they watch you neglect yourself and your basic hygiene and happiness for years, they will assume that is what's expected of them. If you struggle to get your child to brush their teeth but do not regularly brush your own, what good is your word? The example you set for your children in their new home will be the standard by which they define themselves going forward.

Do not neglect yourself for your children, because the only result will be your children learning your same neglect-based tendencies.

Reflection Questions:

1. List three things you do that make you feel more human. It can be anything from pedicures to lying in bed for 15 minutes before getting up. If you can think of more, list more.
2. Go through that list and write down beside each item how many times a week that task should be performed.
3. What can you do to make sure at least two of those tasks are worked into your schedule on a regular basis?

Chapter Nine:
USEFUL ADVICE

Sometimes, you are simply lost. In a world that bases its answers to the community in scientific facts and physical evidence, it can be hard to draw necessary knowledge from within yourself in order to navigate unknown territory. Separation and divorces are hardly things that come with precedence, and even if someone has been through more than one, no one scenario is ever the same. In this regard, sometimes it is simply innate to turn to those that have warred the path you are about to travel and seek out their personal advice based on their own experiences.

There are women out there that are easily reachable. Technology and social media groups have made it possible to connect with people just like us who are in or have gone through similar situations. This knowledge stems beyond what a court mandates you to understand. Mandated parenting classes teach the separating spouses things like not talking bad of the other parent in front of the children and never making them the middleman delivery system for messages between you two. And, while that is wonderful advice, there is much that is lacking about many other facets of this journey.

How do you navigate it? How do you stop being angry? Where do you go from here? Are there resources at your disposal?

Here is an easily digestible list of all the advice single mothers out there want you to know while you are going through this process. Things they wished they would have known while they were dealing with it themselves.

It's alright to be angry. It is not alright to be angry at your children for not being angry at your ex-spouse. Your relationship with your ex does not have any bearing on the relationship they will cultivate with them, unless you are coming from an abuse scenario.

Find productive ways to get rid of your anger: exercise, scream in the shower, cry to a friend, ritualistically burn pictures of your ex-spouse in a fireplace. Do whatever you need to do to expel that anger. Then? Get rid of it. It will only hold you back.

Make trips across state lines fun for the kids. Stop at a hotel with a pool and let them swim. Let them have a big bowl of ice cream in their hotel bed. Let them fall asleep watching television. If the trek to and from each parent's home is seen as adventurous and fun, it will start their transition off just fine. If it's filled with tension and unease, your children will be emotional about the trade-off.

Children who are younger than four will never remember the moment the two of you parted. They will not remember that one parent walking out, and they will not remember the arguments the two of you had while the child was "sleeping." They will, however, remember the broken promises and lack of contact as they grow older. Do not let your damaged relationship with the other parent impede on your ability to keep in touch with and keep up with your own child.

Your children are not pawns. Period.

Food preparation saved my life. Make your own freezer meals. It's a homemade dinner that requires some oven heating, and that's it.

Family nights are still important even in split homes. Carve out a night with your kids where the outside world doesn't impede. Order pizza. Watch a movie. Play a board game. Go out somewhere and explore. Family time is more important now than it ever was.

It is possible to raise stable children in a divorced household. Wanna know how you do it? Just like you would in a forged home: co-parent with respect, don't badmouth the children's other parent in front of them, and stop grilling them about what they did when they were with them. Seriously. Stop.

Prep everything: get a coffee pot that makes coffee at a designated time in the morning. Prep dinners so they only need to be heated. Lay out your outfit for the next day. Pack your child's lunches the day prior. If you are a control freak, it will help give you some semblance of control back. Plus, it frees up time to further unwind. Less stress is always a good thing.

You will get lonely. Prepare yourself for it. And when it happens, have someone you can call. Not so they can come over, but so they can talk with you. Filling your loneliness with meaningless sex will do you no good.

You are not a failure. It is not simply your fault. It takes two to make a marriage and two to break a marriage. Understand that you are not completely at fault, but you are not completely innocent, either. Unless the situation is abusive. There's no need for that crap. Ever

It's not an easy process, but it is a survivable one.

Time doesn't heal all things. That's bull. What does heal things is distance. The longer you live without your spouse, and the more time is put between you and this event, the easier things will become.

Give yourself time to adjust to your new routine. Be kind to yourself.

If throwing the gifts your spouse gave you in the garbage helps, then do it. If clutching onto them while crying at 2 AM will help you, do it. There is no right or wrong way to cope, unless it begins to physically hurt someone. Don't let anyone tell you how to cope. Only you will know how to cope.

Do not announce it until you are ready to talk about, and when you do? Be ready for the barrage of questions, because they are coming.

I hate the term "broken home." Your children are not from a "broken home," they are from an "improved home." Staying with someone who is toxic breeds anger and resentment, and it's not healthy for kids to grow up in that environment.

Above all else: know that you're not alone.

Chapter Ten:
YOU WILL MAKE IT

Understand this: Divorce is not a life sentence. What this means is that you will make it and you will come out stronger because of it. However, the determining factor for that strength is how willing you are to pedal forward despite the possibility of wanting to hold onto the past. For any person in any situation, grieving for the past is normal. It is a part of your life that existed for so long, and how you have been thrust into a situation that is not only new, but lonely.

Understand, you will be alright.

How do I know this? Well, because I've been through it. I have fought the battle of finding a job after years of being a stay-at-home housewife. I have fought the battle of watching my spouse move out of the house. I have fought the questions on how to make this transition fun for my child, and I have fought the uphill battle of having no workforce experience and suddenly needing a job. Rest assured, the greatest untapped force on this planet is the ferocity of a single mother needing to provide for her children. Tap into that frustration and turn it into a way to show your spouse exactly what they neglected. Take that anger and fuel it into carving a future out for yourself and your children.

You cannot allow this process to drown you.

If your ex-spouse is completely out of the situation, whether they have passed on or have proven to be an incompetent parent, then the responsibility has multiplied. The stress had been added on and your roles in your children's lives has just grown exponentially. Yes, this is overwhelming and you can feel that way, but that is why making sure you have a well-thought-out plan is imperative. If you are having sleepless nights you cannot combat, use that time to do research and look for jobs you might be interested in. If you find yourself unable to do much, then sit on the couch and rest while researching different federal aids in your area. Many single mothers find themselves using federal support to take care of their families, and there is nothing wrong with this. Those programs are there to help people like us during transitions just like this.

The positive choices you make going forward will forever cement the overall health of your children. Understand that you cannot control how your ex-spouse will react to things, but you can control how you react. They will watch you and they will learn from you, and as they grow older they will come to respect the dignity and calm demeanor you had throughout this entire process. But, not only will they watch your reactions, but they will watch your actions, and this is why taking care of yourself in so important. To handle the stress that comes with being a single mother, you should make sure you have ways of coping healthily with your stress. To teach your children how to cope with the things life will throw at them, you must understand how the process of coping with stress works.

Start with yourself and you will provide your children with a visual explanation before they are even able to communicate verbally with you.

You are more than just a mother now. You are a financial supporter, mental caretaker, physical anchor, and the glue that now holds you and your children together. Taking care of yourself means taking care of the very foundation of your new familial dynamic. If you don't, the very foundation of your children's world becomes rocked, and with that sensation comes many different emotions that they may or may not be able to cope with, depending on what you have emulated to them.

Make use of them.

The greatest thing you can do for yourself is to find a group of women similar to yourself. Many online social media groups and neighborhood church organizations have programs that not only benefit single mothers, but bring them together in a safe environment so their children can play and they can talk to others in their position. Simply having that time where your children socialize and you talk with others who are like you can be cathartic and reassuring. Many of these people will be more advanced in their situations than you, and you can get a real-life glimpse into the fact that you will be alright.

Not only that, but many of these women hold incredible advice as well as services to take advantage of that you might not have thought of or realized yet.

Even more of a benefit, however? Many of these in-person organizations are up-to-date with businesses in the area that seek to hire single mothers who are supporting their children, and your new status can be the foot in the door you need in order to secure an interview for a job.

Divorce is hard to do, but not impossible to overcome. Do not allow this shock to your system to drain you of the life-force that will be necessary to take care of your children. Get out and experience the world around you. Dive into aspects of your life you would have never imagined otherwise. Use this as a clean slate instead of viewing it as a life sentence. If you are happy, you will grow a happy family.

And that is the most vital part of this entire process.

Reflection Questions:

1. Go stand in the mirror and take a good, hard look at yourself.
2. Draw in a deep breath through your nose before letting it out slowly from your mouth.
3. Now, look yourself in the eyes and repeat these words four times: "I will make it."

www.ingramcontent.com/pod-product-compliance
Lightning Source LLC
Chambersburg PA
CBHW071748020426
42331CB00008B/2222